Basic Tools & Supplies

Rubber Stamps, Ink Pads, Colored Markers

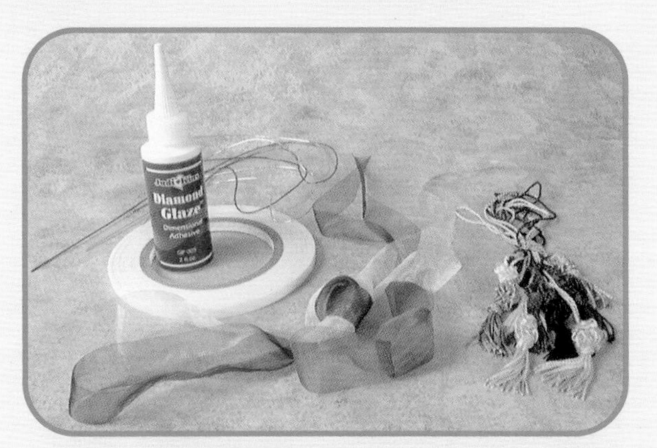

Glue, Adhesive Tape and Accessories

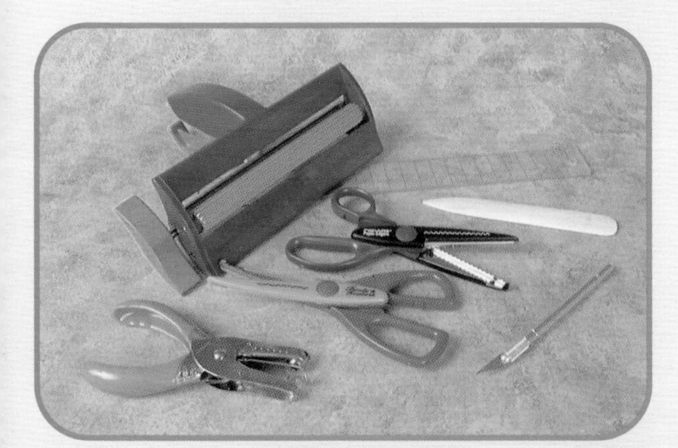

Crimping Tool, Wavy Scissors, Paper Punch

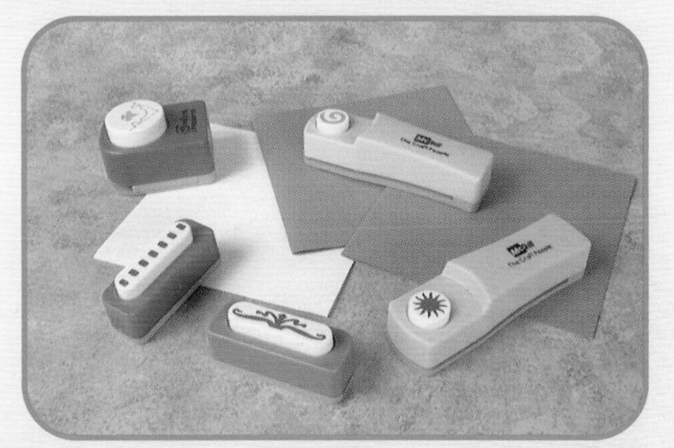

Paper Punches & Colored Cardstock Paper

Table of Contents

Vellum with Rubber Stamping II *pictures unique designs for creating with paper. Over 36 different projects and Rubber Stamping techniques turn Vellum translucent parchment paper and elegant cardstock into some of the most elegant and unusual card designs I've ever seen.*

A NOTE ABOUT VELLUM ACIDITY
Vellum papers are very close to neutral pH levels. When using Vellum, we recommend protecting your photos by placing acid-free cardstock between your photos and Vellum paper.
Acidity Level of Vellum paper used in this book. (#1 - 6.04, #2 - 5.53, #3 - 5.68)

pj dutton

pj dutton lives in Festus, Missouri. She has been creating samples for Judi-Kins for the past few years. pj teaches in the St. Louis area and across the country at conventions and rubber stamp stores. pj is a regularly featured artist in THE RUBBER STAMPER magazine and has appeared in SOMERSET STUDIO and RUBBERSTAMPMADNESS.

EXPRESS
PLORE
UME
perimENT
X
CA
95448
P.O. Bo
2425

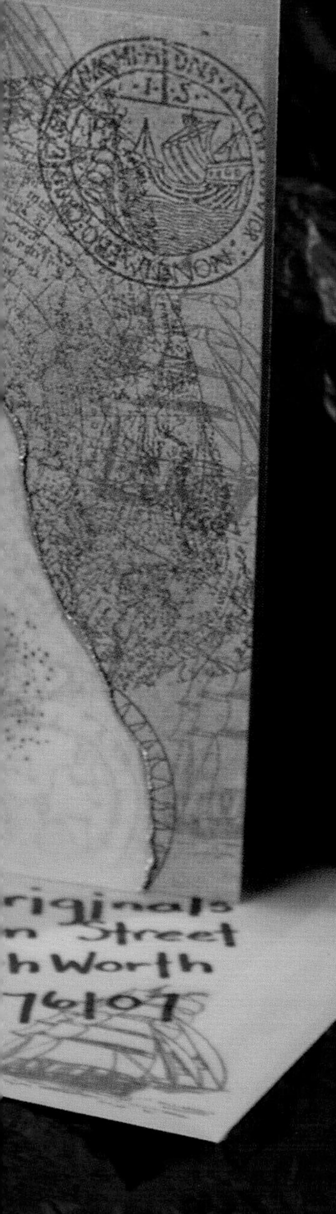

Sun Collage

MATERIALS: Toybox world map, cosmic sun, ancient eclipse and moon faces rubber stamps • 8½" x 5½" piece of vellum • 4" x 5" piece of lightweight vellum • 3⅜" x 4¾" Blueberry card • Two 4¼"x 5½" pieces of Cream cardstock • Forget Me Not square card and envelope • Grey, Turquoise, Light Blue, Yellow, Prussian Blue, Light Green, Pale Orange and Black dye base ink • Photo corner punch • Stipple brush

INSTRUCTIONS: Stamp Prussian Blue cosmic sun on vellum, let dry. Trim around edges of image. Stamp Black map on one piece of Cream cardstock. Color with inks using stipple brush. Trim around edges of image. Punch corners on Blueberry card. Slip cardstock and vellum into photo corners. Trim remaining Cream cardstock to 4⅞" x 3½". Center and glue Blueberry card on Cream cardstock. Stamp Grey maps on square card. Stamp Prussian Blue moon phases and eclipses randomly. Tape cosmic sun piece to front of square card. Stamp envelope to match square card.

Express

MATERIALS: Zettiology express and Acey Deucy goddess cartouche, medallion, text, quest and planet gaze rubber stamps • 4¼" x 5½" piece of lightweight vellum • 5½" x 8½" piece of Birch cardstock • 4¼" x 5½" piece of Cream cardstock • 4¼" x 5½" piece of newsprint • Design Originals vellum envelope • Pale Orange, Ochre, Light Green, Light Blue, Brown and Dark Brown dye base • Post-it notes • Stipple paintbrush • Round corner punch • Deckle edge scissors • 1/16" hole punch • Brown yarn

INSTRUCTIONS: Score and fold cardstock. Holding newsprint and vellum together, cut around edges with deckle scissors. Stamp Dark Brown express in center of vellum. Place newsprint on Cream cardstock and stamp Brown goddess cartouche border. Remove newsprint. Stamp Dark Brown quest on upper left and planet gaze on lower right corner and on Post-it notes. Cut out designs on Post-it notes and place over stamped images to mask. Stamp Brown medallion and text several times on card. Remove masks and stipple images and border using dye base inks. Trim cardstock to 4" x 5¼" and punch round corners. Stack cardstock and vellum on front of card. Punch 2 holes in top of card and tie with yarn. Stamp envelope as shown in photo.

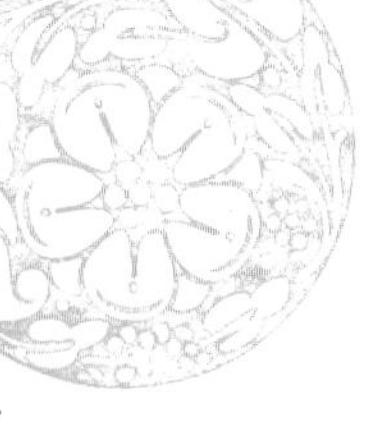

Ship

MATERIALS: Judi-Kins sky and Toybox large polar view map, faciat seal, sun world and ship rubber stamps • 8½" x 5½" piece of heavyweight vellum • 8½" x 5½" piece of kraft cardstock • Colored pencils • Light Green, Light Blue, Brown and Plum dye base inks • Stipple brush • Clear embossing ink • Metallic Bronze embossing powder • Heat tool • Double sided tape

INSTRUCTIONS: Score and fold cardstock and vellum. Stamp Dark Brown map, seal and sun world on front of cardstock. Stamp 3 Brown ships. Stipple Light Blue, Light Green and Plum. Stamp Dark Brown ship on vellum as shown in photo. Stamp Light Blue sky for water. Color back of ship with pencils. Starting at top, tear vellum diagonally from left to right. Drag torn edge in embossing ink, emboss. Apply tape to back edge of fold on cardstock and attach vellum. Apply ⅛" double sided tape to left side of vellum, sprinkle with embossing powder and emboss. Stamp 3 Brown ships along bottom of envelope.

Stamped Overlays

Stamped & colored designs beneath a Vellum overlay give a subtle opulence to handmade cards.

1. Make card. Trim Vellum with decorative edge scissors.

2. Stamp first images. Mask with Post-it notes and stamp remaining images.

3. Lightly color card with various colors of ink.

ART
play
dream
passion
1305
festus,

Embossing

Embossing

Simply stamp Vellum with embossing powder, heat to emboss and add color for elegantly finished cards.

Art Deco

MATERIALS: Paula Best creative words cube and Judi-Kins deco square rubber stamps • 3½" square of heavyweight vellum • Sage square card and matching envelope • Black pigment ink • Black Opal embossing powder • Watercolor markers • Heat tool • Long reach swirl punch • Deckle edge scissors

INSTRUCTIONS: Stamp deco square on vellum, emboss. Color back of image with markers. Trim edges with deckle scissors. Place vellum on front of card and lightly mark corners with a pencil. Punch swirls on pencil marks. Stamp words on card, emboss. Color with markers. Slip corners of vellum into punched swirls. Stamp envelope as shown in photo, color with markers.

Initial Window Card

MATERIALS: Judi-Kins illuminated alphabet and stitched background rubber stamps • 5" square of heavyweight vellum • Oregano square card and matching envelope • Dark Green marker • Black pigment ink • Malachite embossing powder • Heat tool • Double sided tape • Post-it tape • Craft knife

INSTRUCTIONS: Stamp initials, emboss and color with marker. Measure and mark 1" frame around initials. Cut out using craft knife being careful to not cut the stamped images. Outline frame with marker. Stamp vellum with stitched background, emboss. Trim vellum to overlap the window opening and tape in place with embossing facing front of card. Mask envelope with Post-it tape leaving 1" at top and bottom. Stamp envelope as shown in photo, emboss. Draw lines with marker. Optional: Cut a ¾" wide frame from a 5¼" square of cardstock to cover edges of vellum on inside of card. Tape in place.

Keys to Art

MATERIALS: Judi-Kins 3 key designs and artists' signature rubber stamps • 8½" x 5½" piece of heavyweight vellum • 11" x 5½" Clay Pot cardstock • Dark Brown dye base ink • Black pigment ink • Metallic Bronze embossing powder • Heat tool • Round corner punch • Double sided tape

INSTRUCTIONS: Score and fold cardstock and vellum. Stamp Dark Brown artists' signatures on front of cardstock aligning stamp with left fold. Punch round corners on right edge. Measure 1¼" from right edge, score and fold to front. Trim 1¼" from the right edge off back of card. Punch round corners on folded edge. Apply tape to back edge of front fold on cardstock and attach vellum. Stamp keys as shown in photo, emboss.

1 Stamp design on Vellum using embossing ink.

2 Sprinkle design with embossing powder, brush off excess powder.

3 Heat to emboss. Color design with watercolor markers.

You are loved

Crimping

Crimping is an easy way to add unique texture to your Vellum creations. The crimping tool makes it quick and easy.

You are Loved

MATERIALS: Magenta flower border and That's All She Stamped 'You are loved' rubber stamps • 4¼" x 5½" piece of lightweight vellum • 8½" x 5½" piece of MatteKote cardstock • Plum dye base ink • Fiskars paper crimper • ⅛" hole punch • 18" of ⅞" Pink sheer ribbon

INSTRUCTIONS: Score and fold cardstock. Stamp flower border across center front of card and across top and bottom edges of vellum. Stamp 'You are loved' between borders on vellum. Place bottom edge of vellum in crimper, crimp for 1" and remove. Repeat for top edge. Place vellum on card and punch 2 holes through vellum and front of card. Thread ribbon down through left hole and up through right hole, down through left, up through right, pull gently to tighten. Trim tails. Stamp envelope to match card.

Key to My Heart

MATERIALS: Carmen's Veranda key, Magenta floral heart and Judi-Kins Q-bit heart rubber stamps • 8½" x 5½" piece of heavyweight vellum • 8½" x 5½" piece of Forget-Me-Not cardstock • Design Originals vellum envelope • Prussian Blue dye base ink • Black pigment ink • Antique Lead embossing powder • Heat tool • Grey marker • Postage edge scissors • Small Silver tassel with slide • Fiskars paper crimper

INSTRUCTIONS: Score and fold vellum and cardstock. Stamp 9 Prussian Blue Q-bit hearts 1" from bottom and floral heart on right side of cardstock. Stamp key on vellum using pigment ink, emboss. Color back of key with marker. Trim bottom edge of vellum with postage scissors. Crimp 1" along bottom edge. Slide vellum over cardstock and secure with tassel. Stamp Prussian Blue floral heart on bottom left of envelope.

Kimono

MATERIALS: Judi-Kins bamboo kimono and Japanese background rubber stamps • 8½" x 5½" piece of lightweight vellum • 8½" x 5½" piece of Birch cardstock • Design Originals vellum envelope • Dark Brown dye base ink • Black pigment ink • Metallic Bronze embossing powder • Heat tool • Small Ivory tassel with slide • Fiskars paper crimper

INSTRUCTIONS: Score and fold cardstock. Stamp Dark Brown background on front of cardstock. Crimp center 3" of vellum. Score and fold vellum. Stamp kimono on center right of vellum using pigment ink, emboss. Slide vellum over cardstock and secure with tassel. Stamp Dark Brown background on envelope as shown in photo.

1. Stamp design on card.

2. Stamp designs on vellum.

3. After ink is dry, crimp Vellum.

Gift Tags

Handmade, one-of-a-kind Vellum gift tags are the perfect way to make all your gifts say, 'You're very special'.

1 Stamp design on Vellum. Score fold line using a ball tip stylus.

2 Cut out design leaving folded edge uncut.

3 Color back of design using watercolor markers.

Surprise Package
MATERIALS: Judi-Kins package rubber stamp • 6½" x 3½" piece of heavyweight vellum • Black pigment ink • Black embossing powder • Heat tool • Watercolor markers
INSTRUCTIONS: Stamp package on right edge of vellum, emboss. Score and fold along left edge of package. Cut around package. Color on back with markers.

Deco Wreath
MATERIALS: Judi-Kins deco wreath rubber stamp • 6½" x 3½" piece of heavyweight vellum • Black pigment ink • Malachite embossing powder • Heat tool • Watercolor markers
INSTRUCTIONS: Stamp wreath on right edge of vellum, emboss. Score and fold along left edge of wreath. Cut around wreath. Color on back with markers.

Conversation Hearts
MATERIALS: Carmen's Veranda box of hearts and Valentine's hearts cube rubber stamps • 6½" x 3½" piece of heavyweight vellum • Light Blue dye base ink • Black pigment ink • Black embossing powder • Heat tool • Watercolor markers
INSTRUCTIONS: Stamp box on right edge of vellum, emboss. Score and fold along left edge of box. Cut around box. Color on back with markers. Stamp Light Blue Valentine's heart on inside centered under front heart. Color on back with markers.

Heart of Love
MATERIALS: Judi-Kins swirl heart frame and Printworks 'Love' rubber stamps • 7½" x 4" piece of heavyweight vellum • Black pigment ink • Gold embossing powder • Heat tool • Red watercolor marker • 1/16" hole punch • Scallop edge scissors • 6" of fine Gold cord
INSTRUCTIONS: Stamp heart on bottom half of vellum, emboss. Score and fold along top edge of heart. Cut around heart. Color on back with marker. Punch hole in top left curve of heart, thread cord through hole and tie ends in a knot.

Ephemera
MATERIALS: Acey Deucy ephemera rubber stamp • 4" x 3" piece of heavyweight vellum • Black dye base ink • Postage edge scissors • Watercolor markers • 1/16" hole punch • 6" of fine Ivory cord
INSTRUCTIONS: Stamp design on right edge of vellum. Score and fold along left edge of image. Cut around image. Color on back with markers. Punch hole in top left corner, thread cord through hole and tie ends in a knot.

Conversation
Hearts
Love

CUT-OUTS

Windows cut in Vellum let the richly colored backgrounds shine in these exquisite card designs.

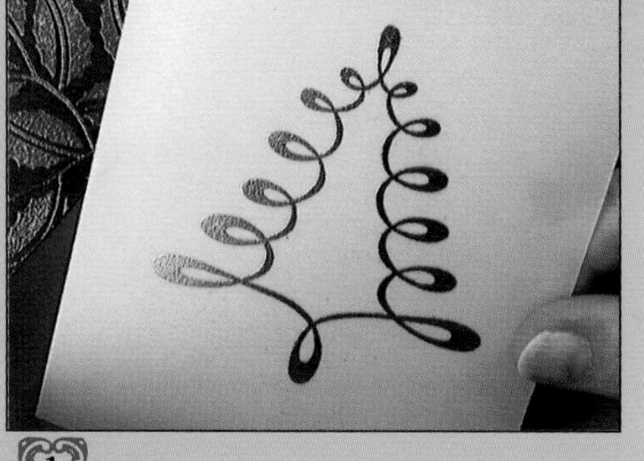

1 Stamp design on Vellum and emboss.

2 Carefully cut out center of design with craft knife.

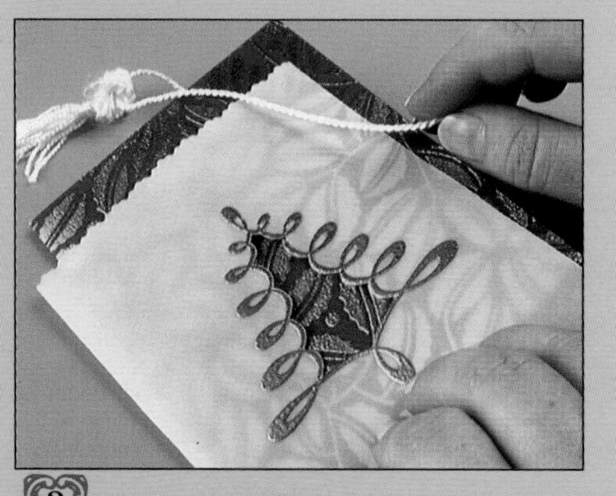

3 Place Vellum cut-out over a stamped and embossed card.

'Love'

MATERIALS: Judi-Kins checkered heart and checkered border and Printworks 'love' rubber stamps • 11" x 5½" piece of heavyweight vellum • 11" x 5½" piece of Blueberry cardstock • Black pigment ink • Lapis Lazuli embossing powder • Heat tool • Craft knife • White shrink plastic • Clearsnap Midnight crafter's ink • Double sided tape

INSTRUCTIONS: Score and fold vellum and cardstock. Stamp borders and heart on vellum, emboss. Cut out center of heart. Apply tape to back edge of fold on Blueberry card and attach vellum. Stamp checkered heart on plastic with crafter's ink which will stay wet until heated. Shrink plastic following manufacturer's instructions. Glue plastic heart on Blueberry cardstock in center of cut out heart.

Autumn Leaves

MATERIALS: Paula Best leaf rubber stamp • 8½" x 5½" piece of heavyweight vellum • 8½" x 5½" piece of Sage cardstock • Black pigment ink • Malachite embossing powder • Heat tool • Craft knife • Victorian edge scissors • Aquacolor crayons • Paintbrush • 18" of ⅞" sheer Green ribbon

INSTRUCTIONS: Score and fold vellum and cardstock. Stamp leaf repeatedly on cardstock, emboss. Color leaves with crayons and blend colors with wet paintbrush. Stamp leaves repeatedly on vellum, emboss. Color leaves on back with crayon and blend colors with wet paintbrush. Cut out interior areas of center leaf with craft knife. Trim edges of vellum with Victorian scissors. Slip vellum over card and secure with ribbon.

Christmas Tree

MATERIALS: Judi-Kins Christmas tree and holly background rubber stamps • 8¼" x 5½" piece of heavyweight marbled vellum for cover • 8½" x 5½" piece of Dark Green cardstock • Black pigment ink • Gold embossing powder • Heat tool • Craft knife • Scallop edge scissors • Small White tassel with slide

INSTRUCTIONS: Score and fold vellum and cardstock. Stamp holly background on front of cardstock, emboss. Stamp tree on center front of vellum, emboss. Cut out center of tree. Slip vellum over card and secure with tassel.

love

Pear

MATERIALS: Stampers Anonymous script and pear rubber stamps • 8½" x 5½" piece of lightweight vellum • 11" x 5½" piece of Sage cardstock • 4¼" x 5½" piece of Cream cardstock • Green and Yellow dye base ink • Foil glue • Gold foil • Stipple brush • Gold tassel with slide • Double sided tape

INSTRUCTIONS: Score and fold cardstock and vellum. Score and fold cardstock 1¼" from right edge and fold to front, trim 1¼" off back of card. Stamp Green script to cover front of cardstock. Stamp Yellow pear repeatedly on front of vellum. Tape vellum under cardstock flap. Slide tassel on card and tighten. Stamp Green pear on Cream cardstock, stipple Yellow. Apply glue to pear edges, let dry until clear. Rub foil on glue. Cut out pear and tape on front of vellum.

Roman Feast

MATERIALS: Stampers Anonymous Roman feast, Roman numerals and script rubber stamps • 4" square of lightweight vellum • 11" x 5½" piece of Sage cardstock • Green dye base ink • Gold pigment ink • Watercolor markers • Foil glue • Gold foil • 4 Gold photo corners • Deckle edge scissors

INSTRUCTIONS: Score and fold cardstock. Stamp Green script at different angles to cover front of cardstock. Stamp Gold Roman numerals around border. Stamp Green Roman feast on vellum. Color on back with markers and trim edges with deckle scissors. Apply glue to spiral, let dry until clear. Rub foil on glue. Mount vellum on card with photo corners.

Garden Spot

MATERIALS: Judi-Kins garden spot rubber stamp • 8½" x 5½" piece of heavyweight vellum • 8½" x 5½" piece of Matte Black cardstock • Black pigment ink • Black embossing powder • Heat tool • Foil glue • Gold, Silver and Copper foil • 1/8" hole punch • Victorian decorative edge scissors • 12" of 7/8" sheer Gold ribbon

INSTRUCTIONS: Score and fold vellum and cardstock. Stamp garden spot in center of vellum, emboss. Apply foil glue, let dry until clear. Rub Gold foil on petals, Copper foil on leaves and Silver foil on berries. Trim bottom of vellum with Victorian scissors. Slip vellum over cardstock, punch 2 holes in fold and secure with ribbon.

Add glitz and glitter to all your Vellum creations with beautiful metallic foil. It's a quick and easy way to glamorous color !

1 Stamp design and sprinkle with embossing powder. Heat to emboss.

2 Apply foiling glue to design, let dry until clear.

3 Place dull side of foil on glue and rub to transfer color.

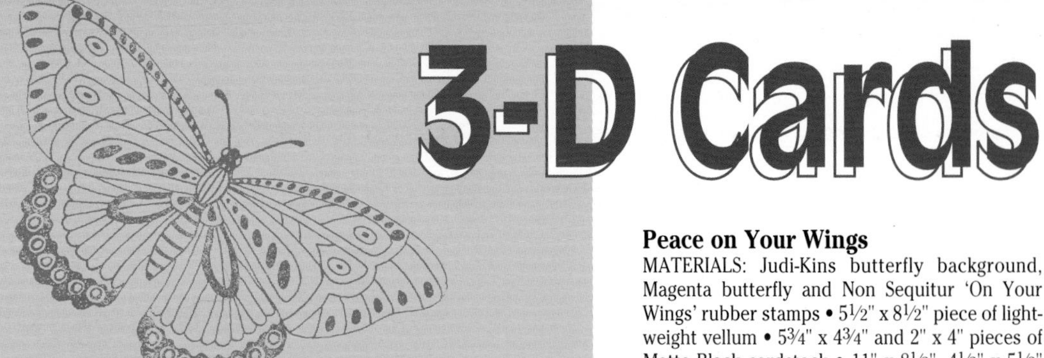

3-D Cards

Bring your cards to life with 3-D Vellum sculptures that pop right off the page.

1 Stamp and color background design on Vellum.

2 Stamp, color and cut out Vellum for 3-D designs.

3 Assemble and glue 3-D pieces. Glue on card.

Peace on Your Wings

MATERIALS: Judi-Kins butterfly background, Magenta butterfly and Non Sequitur 'On Your Wings' rubber stamps • 5½" x 8½" piece of lightweight vellum • 5¾" x 4¾" and 2" x 4" pieces of Matte Black cardstock • 11" x 8½", 4½" x 5½" and 1¾" x 3¾" pieces of White cardstock • Black dye base ink • Black pigment ink • Black Opal embossing powder • Colored pencils • Watercolor markers • Diamond glaze • 5" of Black paper cord • 2 Black seed beads • Design Originals large vellum envelope

INSTRUCTIONS: Score and fold 11" x 8½" piece of cardstock. Stamp butterfly background on 4½" x 5½" piece of White cardstock with dye base ink. Color with pencils. Glue on 5¾" x 4¾" piece of Black cardstock. Stamp 'On Your Wings' on 1¾" x 3¾" piece of White cardstock with pigment ink, emboss. Glue on 2" x 4" piece of Black cardstock. Glue butterfly and 'On Your Wings' pieces on front of card. Stamp butterfly 3 times on vellum with dye base ink. Color first butterfly completely, top set of wings and body on second butterfly and bottom set of wings and body on third butterfly. Cut out colored images. Score wings at the body. Glue bottom set of wings on complete body. Then glue top set of wings in place. Add dimension to body with diamond glaze, let dry. Cut paper cord in half, glue beads on ends and glue to under side of butterfly body. Glue butterfly on front of card. Stamp 3 butterflies on envelope with dye base ink. Color with markers.

Leaves

MATERIALS: Paula Best leaf and fall leaves rubber stamps • 5½" x 8½" and 4¼" x 5½" pieces of heavyweight vellum • 5½" x 8½" piece of White cardstock • Green dye base ink • Black pigment ink • Metallic Bronze embossing powder • Heat tool • Diamond glaze • Watercolor markers • Round corner punch • 1/16" hole punch • 12" of thin Gold cord

INSTRUCTIONS: Score and fold 5½" x 8½" pieces of cardstock and vellum. Stamp Green leaves repeatedly on front of cardstock. Stamp leaves around edge and one in center of vellum with pigment ink, emboss. Color back of leaves with markers. Stamp 2 leaves on 4¼" x 5½" piece of vellum with pigment ink, emboss. Color back of leaves with markers. Cut out leaves, score centers and glue on center of vellum. Slide vellum over cardstock, punch 2 holes in fold and tie with cord. Punch round corners.

Dragonfly

MATERIALS: Rubber Monger dragonfly rubber stamp • 5½" x 8½" and 4¼" x 5½" pieces of lightweight vellum • 5½" x 8½" piece of Fleck cardstock • Prussian Blue and Grey dye base ink • Watercolor markers • Round corner punch • Small Lavender tassel with slide

INSTRUCTIONS: Score and fold 5½" x 8½" pieces of cardstock and vellum. Stamp Grey dragonflies repeatedly on front of cardstock. Stamp Prussian Blue dragonfly on 5½" x 8½" piece of vellum. Color back of dragonfly with markers. Stamp a dragonfly on 4¼" x 5½" piece of vellum, color on back with markers and cut out. Score wings at body, curl wings gently by pulling across blade of scissors and glue on dragonfly stamped on vellum card. Slide vellum over cardstock and secure with tassel. Punch round corners.